The Rigged Universe

The Rigged Universe

poems by Anthony Labriola

Shanti Arts Publishing
Brunswick, Maine

THE RIGGED UNIVERSE

Published by Shanti Arts
93 Hillside Road
Brunswick, Maine 04011
shantiarts.com

Copyright © 2013, 2020 Anthony Labriola
All rights reserved. No part of this book may be used or reproduced in any manner whatsoever without the written permission of the publisher.

First edition published 2013
Second edition 2020

Cover and interior design by Shanti Arts

Cover image, "Ocean Wave," courtesy of the Thomas Bouckley Collection, The Robert McLaughlin Gallery, Oshawa, Ontario, Canada

Scientists have determined that the average color of the universe is a bland "cosmic latte," the color used on the cover.
CMYK (0%, 5.83%, 5.8%, 0%) RGB (255, 240, 240)
https://www.dailymail.co.uk/sciencetech/article-1224865

Printed in the United States of America

ISBN: 978-1-951651-21-3 (softcover)

Library of Congress Control Number: 2013954825

To my mother and father
in admiration and gratitude;

To Josephine
in love and delight;

To our children,
Anthony, Michelle, Nicolas, Christina, and Joanna
in awe and wonder.

Contents

Acknowledgements   11

Rigging the Universe
Tricks of Light   14
The Rigged Universe   15
The Spell   16
Water Torture   17
Magical Thinking   18
Misdirection   19
The Stars Are Dying   20
A Boy Magician   21
Magic Wings   22
Dismantling a Toy Train   23
Black Cat   24
Pigeon   25
Enough to Disappear   26
No Animals Were Harmed   27
Leaving December   28
Wishes and Lullabies   29
Drowning My Book   30
The Love of Complication   31
Remember Me   32
Another Fate   33
Midnight Room   34
Death Is Near   35
Last Wish   36
Magic Words   37
The Scavenger   38
Winter Kept Us Warm   39

Rough Magic

Rough Magic	42
Magic Island	43
Naked Landscapes	47
Exposure	48
Winter Mirage	49
Never in Chains	50
Fragments of the Afternoon	51
Scream Therapy	52
Hunting the Magician	53
Cold Coin	54
Birdsong	55
In the First Person	56
Failure	57
In Twos	58
Emergency Ward	59
The Poet as a Bear	60
Escaping Fate	61
Making Peace	62
Pleading Innocence	63
Making Friends Disappear	64
Don't Go Away Mad	65
Poet with Sunflower	66
She Was Supposed to Die First	67
Street Parade	68
The Subject Is Color	69
Breathing Light	70

Enchantments of the Real World

The Play of the World	74
Appearing in the Wilderness	75

Hunger	76
Motion Sickness	77
Field Notes	78
A Spear Thrown at the Gathering Storm	79
Changing Landscapes	80
Inward Journey	81
Magic Forest	82
Winter Photograph	83
The Farther Away He Journeys	84
The Other Shore	85
Reading the River	86
Walking Naked	88
Arrivals and Departures	89
For Those Who Watch the Wilderness	90
West Coast Messages	91
The Secret Language of the Hunt	92
Winter's Phantoms	93
Substitutions	94
Abandoning the Page	95
Driftwood Fire	96
The Descent	97
Throat Singers of the Animal Kingdom	98
Burning Lake	99
Landscape of Endings	100
Mountain Outlook	101
The First Tree We Ever Climbed	102
Whale Watching	103
Enchantments of the Open Road	104
About the Author	107

Acknowledgements

"Breathing Light" first appeared in *Stone Voices*, 2012. "Tricks of Light" first appeared in *Vallum Magazine*, 2013. "Reading the River" first appeared in *Stone Voices* (online only), 2013. "Escaping Fate" (in a slightly different version) first appeared in *Passion: Poetry*, 2013.

For insights into "the celebration of the mystery of the world" and "the play of the world," I am indebted to my friend and colleague, Chris McBride, and his amazing work on Martin Heidigger.

I am especially indebted to Christine Cote for her enthusiasm to transform the world through art.

Rigging the Universe

Tricks of Light

I track the turning sky with its blaze-bright haloes —
solar and lunar. Mocked by tricks of light,
I'm running with the Sun Dogs, baying with
the Moon Dogs, bursting in and out of sight.

The grand illusionist makes heavenly bodies
appear with or without a wand. Now you see them,
now you don't — the bright smirk of the mock Sun
and the curled lip of the Moon. The sky turns around

and spins me on an astrological wheel
in a cosmic knife-throwing stunt that performs
the trick as if from the act of a mind-freak.

With blazing eyes, the knife-thrower hurtles
long knives to miss the mock targets on purpose
in the misdirection of the magic sky.

The Rigged Universe

A rigged universe with a chance to pull

the strings: a demonstration of how it
all works, how it's all a magic trick,
how deceivers undeceive and magicians

hold up disbelief. Everything is up my sleeve
in real-time links between hand and eye.
The universe doesn't stand a chance when magic

takes over — *Hocus pocus* and a book of spells
with tricky thrills, Shamanic voices, eyes
in the palms of each hand, the wisdom of wizards

and witches, Druidic signs of water
and spirit. I want the real voodoo and what's
behind the curtain, a life-changing offer

in the rigged dark of this night's magic show.

The Spell

No psychology or science to make sense
of the world, only magic. I fall asleep

until the spell is broken. Then levitate.
Sawed in two, my body parts are put together

again. With a snap of his fingers, the mentalist
wakes me from my spell. But there are too many

rising shadows not to be afraid of magic.
A bird inside a light bulb, a silver ball

floating around a cloth, a woman hovering
a few inches off the floor, a black cat shuffling

a deck of cards, never to reveal the secret
of the trick or any illusion. I half-believe

the lie and, in a trance, try to figure it out.
Everywhere I look, the audience is sleeping.

Water Torture

Magic hangs me upside down, like Houdini
in a fish tank. Handcuffed and chained, I attempt
to escape the Chinese Water Torture Cell.

With or without *abracadabra*, rough magic
takes over. With the flashing of a magic wand,
dervishes of light dance in the revolving sky.

No escaping the illusions of grand magic —
apparitions that have me in their thrall.
With blazing eyes, I sink into the tank

and, in my drowning straightjacket, defy death.
Under a hypnotized sun, I spin on
an astrological chart. I take a chance —

a human target splayed on a flashing wheel —
round and round at the command of magic words.

MAGICAL THINKING

The real show is in my head. Magical

thinking improves my chances in a quarrel
with the real world. As a one-eyed magician,
I exchange loss for gain, a dead Elvis

for a sighting, a lost lottery ticket
for the jackpot, the subversion of an empty
top hat for the sudden appearance of rabbits.

But when I'm the mirthless Joker, my nightmare
becomes the moviegoers' massacre.
I missed the *magic bus* of my generation

and lost my seat on the *magical mystery
tour.* Magical thinking threatens
what it can't get with what it takes to claim

a piece of the wishful thinker's magic prize.

Misdirection

I seek illusions that are real, not fake.
Most vanishing acts that make magicians
materialize and dematerialize
are parts of the same process. Quick fingers

perform the eyeless trick. A sleight-of-hand
palms my eyeballs. The magician plucks out
the vile jellies and pockets them. He shows
the world the palm of his empty hand and points.

My eyes become thrill-seekers leaping
into the starless sky. The illusionist
is a shaman, a medicine man, a wood-spirit.

My blind eyes are looking for a new illusion.
A misdirection in seeing and believing —
not a freak of nature that reveals the trick.

The Stars Are Dying

The stars are dying, but it's too soon
to go on about that now — the things
that won't come back — how beautiful the magic
words were when I was young and how they
prepared me without knowing it for this moment
with dying stars. As a lost magician, I live
alone at last, pacing the floor in the upper
room, riding out the night of incantations
with sympathetic magic and enchantments
of the real world. But if I'm not careful,
it will be an old score to settle, dark matter
of resentment, the distinction between
loneliness and paradise — in the form
of a dying star — the memory of light.

A Boy Magician

How things turn out on this side of the seawall

is a higher call. Only what is lost
is ever searched for. Against the universal
laws, as a boy magician, I threw a ball

across the ocean from one landmass to another.
A continent shifted, tilted, then tipped towards me.
I don't know how much you're going to believe

this, but once I stood on a pier in Halifax,
appearing to the new world, suitcase at my side,
arriving. I lost the days that smelled like grapes

away from the vineyard in Southern Italy.
Turned my back on the shimmering Atlantic,
but found the magic continent appearing

before me — shining from sea to sea to sea.

Magic Wings

My drawing hand grips a tiny pencil
like a magic wand. It streaks lickety-split

across my bedroom wall. Behold the child-
artist's hand in full flight. Wild birds

lift off the perch of my pencil. My quick hand
can see in the dark — with an eye in the palm.

But which is quicker — hand or eye that blindly
draws birdlike creatures as large as life —

all plumes, beaks, and bird heads? They crowd the wall
like a murder of crows or a murmuration

of starlings. But other figures escape
from the bird's eye view of my drawing hand.

The walls are now covered with the glare of birds.
Drawn in bright flight, their magic wings unfolding.

Dismantling a Toy Train

Train yard: freight cars, crisscrossing tracks, black smoke.
Soot, shouts and whistles, searing, screeching sounds.

The non-stop, mechanical thumping of
shunting trains. It must be raining, or after —

sweet smell of rain and the stench of smoke rising.
I can almost taste it — diesel oil. I smell

of smoke on hair and skin. I recall the smell.
The worst is over or nearly. I wait

to get it done. Then make my move and pay
the price, give memory its due, perform the trick.

Remembering takes something apart — to know how
it works. My memory dismantles a toy train

to see if I can put it back together again.
Remembered, the commonplace is almost magical.

Black Cat

The magician's assistant is a black cat.
Entranced by the moon phases of her power,
he strokes her tail in sequence. Music plays
for the lingering stages of her magical

indifference. A pick plucked out of her
ivory throat strums the strings of her voice.
She whispers magic words into his shell-like ear.
The enchantment leaves claw marks on his brain

and fur on his thoughts. The black cat laces up
her white figure skates and glides on the ice-bound
double bed. No hisses, no regrets, only

enchanted pirouettes. With the long blades
of her tricked-out claws, she performs her jump
and sticks the landing on the enchanter's head.

Pigeon

I caught a bird: a pigeon in the cage
of my plumed fingers. My brimming hands
felt the pang, ache and twitch of its plump body.
I watched it struggle to live, quivering.

What did I expect: the vibration of fear
or love? The thrill or panic of killing
a living thing? I put the beak to my lips.
It pecked me hard. Blood compelled. The release

came with open hands. Unfolding itself,
shaking off captivity, it winged away.
A fluttering cloud in a slanted sky —
a flying scar on my wounded eyes — there

I was caught in the moment of fright-flight.
But for the uncaught bird, love was freedom.

Enough to Disappear

When the magician's assistant steps through

the mirror, she looks the same in the alternate
reality and blames it on the horoscope —
the magic tweets, the celebrity blog flipping

the bird to the marionette sitting
on her naked lap. When she gets stuck half-in
and half-way out, like Alice through the looking glass,

she hears the magician say: *If you're old enough
to bleed, you're old enough to disappear.*
The negotiations last a lifetime.

The observation is a show trial.
Collapsing into herself like a telescope —
the release comes when she steps through shattered

glass. But when she looks at herself, she isn't there.

No Animals Were Harmed
While Performing this Trick

I'm not on hallucinogens anymore,
the drugs of choice for my generation:
psychedelics, LSD, marijuana,
magic mushrooms. I'm staying clean, just as I
planned to. No syringes or spoons, no hashish
or hookahs, and no powder anywhere
in this desolate house. I knock on wood
when the mad men join the vicious circle.
Now, I feed my head with magic. The magician
has taken away the last vestiges of you.
He's removed every trace, torn up my list
of complaints, and torn you out of my chest.
The bloodletting is over. No animals
were harmed while performing this trick.

Leaving December

Acceptance leads to grace: the possibility
of leaving one moment for the next. In a voice
punished by failure, and to let wonder take over,
I sing the words of one of my son's early songs:

Stay gloriously high in praise. Stay gloriously high . . .
No longer devoted to the magic of words,
I want what's random and free — an end to
manipulation and magic. Let me

choose ordinary possibilities.
Let me step into today every day.
I have to live no matter how or why.
I have to leave December, shrug it off

and move on. I have to accept January
on New Year's Day to transcend yesterday.

Wishes and Lullabies

It is on a day like this that I wish I were
a magician or a cosmic healer to take away

your pain, sick child of the universe.
For your unwished for diagnosis, turn

the body's blunder into wonder —
a wedding day instead of chemotherapy.

To pull the strings behind the cosmic scenes —
to change suffering into a honeymoon —

We suffer because we suffer alone.
The lullaby of peace is our cradle song.

Grant us peace, magicians of life, to heal
our ignorance, the dis-ease of sorrow.

Give cancer to a dying star — no pain
to feel—and not to a child of the universe.

Drowning My Book

The way I accept what is there — objects
that need to be perceived: a stone, a tree,
a field — and what it is to be believed.
The suspension bridge tolerates me
until, in a wavelength of disaster,
it sways, buckles and falls. I fail to accept
it and the unperceived laws of falling.
Tell the bridges that fall — or the towers —
to do it somewhere else, not here and now.
I believe I do not see it and that
it never falls, at least not the way I see it.
When I climb up on the railing to drown
my book of spells, it jumps from my hand
into the ocean, unseen, and swims away.

THE LOVE OF COMPLICATION

I'm not in love with you insofar as
it's about love; complicated to the extent

that it's not real. You like the fact that it's hard.
I skim the surface and you scratch into it.

You itch to find it. I want to get out.
You want to get in, but where is the opening?

If I don't go willingly, then love drags me.
But if I go alone, it gets complicated.

This is the wound that mirrors make, doubting
myself, waiting for the audience to arrive.

You went away when I wasn't there
and came back when I went looking for you.

My unwritten diary is a record
of your absences that complicate the plot.

Remember Me

I let the last chance skip by and missed you.

You missed your chance to abandon the past.
What does it matter to you if I forget you?
I slough off the image of you that must be real

because it seems real. Are you? Are you real?
This is made of paper but memory is made
of dead words — exhalations, unpurified air.

It's not what it seems when it seems what it's not —
the magic of doubling desire and fear.
You look like someone I knew, you whisper.

I'll take a picture of you anyway.
When you escape, it's painfully obvious
that you love me, but can't remember who I am.

So flee from this illusion and remember me.

Another Fate

By accusing you, I accuse myself
of a crime I didn't commit. Guilty
of the charge, I make no denials.
I plead my innocence, victim of a double
vision, realer than the realest murder.
Delusions multiply; negate the feel of the real.
All prophecies are self-fulfilling.
I consult the oracle of my times.
Double down on the crimes of the century.
My eyes are split in two, fragmenting
what I see into what I cannot do.
What doesn't kill me kills the one standing
next to me. I escaped being born.
Now, I try to escape another fate.

Midnight Room

Tempted to tell the truth, the magician
stands in the absolute center of the universe
and disowns the known world. He steps back
into midnight, afraid of the place now.

It trembles, like a dark cell, a tomb,
or a funeral boat that promises
to transport him to the sweet hereafter.
At midnight, all prophets are self-fulfilled.

Yet, in his midnight room, tonight is just too soon.
He shies away from mercy and how it kills.
In the autobiography of a dying wizard,

he has to write this in order to turn
away and never talk about it again —
the way a Druid speaks about love.

Death Is Near

Death is near, like a black feather, fluttering
in darkness. Footsteps falter on the midnight stairs.
A magician's cat is in the way.
From a high window, moonlight floods the listening

room. In ghost light, someone utters the word: *doom*.
Perhaps, it is a little girl dressed in black lace.
She is wearing black lipstick. A tongue-ring
pierces the tip of her tongue. She speaks moon-

whispered words, blinded by a solar eclipse.
Death sent her here to find me and when she draws near
to light the candle, the passageway is lit

for my last rites. A lamplighter's single image
remains: a phosphorous flame. Like a bird
in the house, it announces that death is near.

Last Wish

Masked, a conjurer reveals the trick.
A fortune teller reads the cards — an ocean voyage.
But the last wish cries out: *Show us the trick
of living.* Signs in the sun, moon and stars,

the coffin with its shroud sails drifts on the waves.
But you should have planted bottles
of whiskey beneath the ash tree and buried
my sandals in the dirt to double-cross death.

You should have rammed my blackthorn walking stick
into blood-lisping ground to mark the place.
You should have tossed my hat to the four winds —

a transatlantic bird, the arc of a life
across the tragic sky. Let me rest, old friend,
cradled in the memory I deserve.

Magic Words

How many nights do I call the moon a witch?
Wasps and wild bees pollinate my flowering
words — bittersweet syllables on my tongue.
But I break my staff and repeat what the wizard
wants me to say: *God's country is everywhere.*
In nature's court, they prosecute me
for the damage done to the magic of words.
The jury is still out, but I'm condemned.
Blindfolded, I accuse my accusers
and refuse to escape. I reject nothing,
but accept it all. A black cat crosses
my path with a loaded gun. A magic
bullet speeds along the trajectory, altering
history, and wounding love's mythology.

The Scavenger

Not that I failed, but erred, made mistakes
in my scavenging of gains and losses.
Perhaps, I was defeated as a way
of surviving — that in the city, there is
something more to it than beauty or bloodshed.
Beyond all margins of a double locution,
or tripling in diminishing returns
in the dumpster — the city's lost and found —
the urban landscape is littered with recycling
bins for raccoons and rats to feast on.
And when I dive in to find one man's treasure,
picking up the lost pieces from the trash,
I unspool the string to find my way back,
still reeling from the frenzy of the maze.

Winter Kept Us Warm

Since I was already on death's road,
and all the magic shadows were facing me,
looking for balloons twisted into animals,
I heard one of them say, *Love is not transmitted*

by a stolen kiss. And another was
saying, *In life, you never get out alive.*
She was practising the trick of disappearing.
Her breath formed a tail of smoke in the air,

and her gesture chilled me to the bone. Where was
the heat an old magician needs in his denial
of death? All I could do was show her a card trick.

She chose the Queen of Spades. No goodbye kiss,
I braved the cold. As we passed by each
other on death's road, winter kept us warm.

Rough Magic

Rough Magic

Presto — I awake to find the visible world
changing what I see into what I believe.

Daylight sends out its invitation to see
the world as wonder made visible. *Presto* —

I appear to disappear. This vanishing act
takes place on nature's stage, the universal

theater. What separates me from this appearance
is rough magic that won't give up on the wonder

of seeing what's there and won't budge an inch
on the trick of believing. Applause is heard

at the beginning but missed at the end
of the show. *Presto* — a baby cries. An old man

dies. A spell is cast. Birth cry and death rattle
conjure life's magical day and night. *Presto*

Magic Island

1
Masked, a conjurer reveals the trick.
A fortune teller reads the cards — an ocean
voyage. Reading ocean surface waves,
she charts where our ship has been. The migrant
vessel bears the dead weight of our departure.
Trafficking wind-forces thwart our escape.
From Indian Ocean to Pacific shore,
the captain calls us cargo — wrack and spawn.
Children collect shipwrecked coins from the waves;
upend a bucket, but their coiled rope
snaps in two. Sea-wracked weeks on board — we sleep
and wake to the rise and fall of a bamboo flute.
Shouted down by sailors, wind-wrangled voices
cry out: *Show us the trick of dying.*

2

A sound-bone echoes from the calling deep.
By sailing to a new land, our voyage
doubles for a second chance. In summer's
efflorescence, we behold opposites at play.
Geographical dreams reflect coastlines
on ancient maps of the world. We're standing
before an oceanic riddle. Facing it,
we try to solve the puzzle of the waves.
Our striving roots us to the spot. We're caught
between two guiding stars, two atmospheres —
new land and homeland. In the pull of one pole
and the push of the other: *things-to-come.*
Pelagic birds squawk and talk of salvage.
Red sky at dawn startles the Pacific coast.

3

I measure distances with my nervous
system, as if my brain is on the outside
of my skull. Ocean silence deepens;
plummets sounds — the depths of one tectonic
plate into another. The farther
I journey, the closer I come to knowing.
Will they separate me from you and send me
back or keep me? Stopped, held, put in my place,
questioned, turned away. The law hovers over
my head like a prophecy. Sailing towards
the harbor, gestures extend into a life.
I encroach, moment by moment, coming here.
It becomes another country from the one
I once imagined. The new world is *here*.

4

I try not to let it get to me — stunned
by the August sunlight of the w-e-s-t-c-o-a-s-t.
I watch the whales near the magic island.
Then trudge on — wrack and spawn; still human.
I follow the shadows of wolverines.
Off Vancouver Island, the sunlit harbor
sails towards me. I drift with reflections.
The ship I leave behind is a ghost ship.
One journey ends, another begins —
to end here is not the end in dotted harbor lights.
Flanked by seabirds, I shamble off the roped deck —
interlocking links in an animal chain.
I hear the ocean surface waves,
singing: *This is a safe harbor.*

Naked Landscapes

The fields are buried beneath ice formations.

Here and there, lost in stark, tricked-out landscapes
the remains of dead trees are stripped bare.
Lashed by vile wind, their skinless branches,

gnarled and twisted, barely hold on, hinged
to their black trunks. Mounds jut out of the ground,
like polar bears. Islands dot the blind expanse

of a vast, polar sea; a sea of black glass.
Everything is caught, suspended in ice.
Prevailing, unchanging, the land is desolate —

forbidding in scant light. Escape routes
are still unknown to strangers in this season.
And the coast road is hidden by drifting snow

that dresses the naked landscapes in white robes.

Exposure

Accustomed to mountain storms, my father
loved chasing them. His work on the railway
took him across the Pacific North West.
He wanted to expose me to this place,

but through his eyes. Beyond talk of survival,
he read the Canadian wilderness
with foreign eyes. His homeland had a she-wolf
in the founding of Rome. When he died,

I buried him in the garden, lowered him
down into a cradle of dirt. Before he passed,
he exposed the miracle of where we lived.

I stare at the ocean which exposes
the miracle of the visible world.
The surge of waves shrugs off the past.

Winter Mirage

The question of survival has a way
of forcing you to get along with strangers.
An enchanter renounces control and dances
with his long shadow on the wall.
A peacemaker suddenly makes for the wilds
to negotiate peace with the animals.
An explorer is lost, frozen to death
on a doomed expedition. Winter doesn't
set the day for the execution, but carries
it out. I want to be remembered, to be
pieced back together, like someone returning
after years of ghostly wandering, seeking
the winter sun, like Franklin's specter
caught and covered in fur; winter mirage.

Never in Chains

Hail batters the storm windows. Sleet and wind
tell winter tales. Our winter-haunted house
tries to withstand ceaseless attacks. Beyond this—
something more: a full confession in a raven's

cry; a performance in the sky, singing,
Never in chains. Under my breath, I moan:
No. To hear the sound fade to a whisper
like someone else's voice. The storm is in

my story, and I'm in hers. When I crawl in
beside her, the wind eases and slips off her dress.
I go on talking for the rest of the night.

By dawn, she has changed into a raven—
unchaining her vast wings from dark, lowering
clouds, winging away, like a storm, unbound.

Fragments of the Afternoon

The afternoon falls apart. By the shattered
window, I nest shells and glide my fingernails

across the black table's glittering surface.
In less time than it takes to fragment

the afternoon, I move in the direction
of a private beach. A spider's web

binds my ankles to the wooden steps;
keeps my body away from the hex of the lake.

In slant light, the descending staircase
falls, then plunges into dark waters. The smoke

of last night's fire still devours a piece
of driftwood. Along the shore,

in the sadness of the place, fragments
of the broken afternoon are lost.

Scream Therapy

In my brain, an electrical storm,
a flash fire — an unquiet room.
In scream therapy, screaming is the cure.
Blue herons circle over the treatment center —

Lake Superior's screaming meemies.
I'm screaming in the forest with no wish
to overstay my welcome in a planned escape.
The indifferent day is startled by the hawk

and not the lark. Raven's cry and wolf's howl
sink deep into my throat. Talons and claws
lop off the top of my head, cure me.

With beating wings, fear mauls my hands,
trying to protect my animal face
against the therapy of the screaming forest.

Hunting the Magician

A hunted magician, I write my auto-

biography — how magic is man-
ipulation; a wounding of the eyes,
cheapening of instinct and belief. I'm tired

of the spirit world, of word magic —
the performance that destroys the will.
I step into a box of trees. The river

flashes nearby. The mist covers my escape —
Shimmering light of the fire-fight —
silent fright against the spell of mosquitoes

and black flies. I can't help thinking that
the whole thing is rigged. Tracking dogs are sent out
to bring the escapee back, sink their teeth

into my spine. No trick to disappear.

Cold Coin

I flip a cold coin off the perch of my thumb.
It dazzles in the breathless air of a magical
sky. In defiance of the wounded laws
of gravity, assaulted by wing speed,

the spinning coin soars up to the clouds.
In flight, beyond fantasy, as it breaks free
of the atmosphere, with the thrust of sky-
watchers, bound for outer space, in the whirl-

ing blast-off of heads and tails, it alternates
with the speed of its perpetual spin,
end to end in beginning again and again,

and becomes a tiny UFO, a bright,
spangling star, a pin-prick of silver light —
the coldest coin in the universe.

Birdsong

Up with the early birds this morning,
listening for birdsong at flutter speed —
Last spring, I slept through morning's dazzling
birdsongs, intent on what had gone wrong,

ears plugged with the-end-of-the-world-as-we-know-it.
The din of warring with the banks and creditors
deafened me to the choruses of freedom.
Before the beat of sunrise, choristers

peck, twitter and warble, full-throated,
out of the singing trees. Now, a new chorus
worms its way into my unstopped ears

in leaving the place, and abandoning
the trees, the nesting birds, and their flight,
caught in my hearing as unrecorded birdsong.

In the First Person

Word gets around that they're about to let
me speak in the first person, not the third.
The fear is: I might refuse. And, if I
do, they won't allow me to do it

ever again. That I might speak against
the magic-carpet rides, the blush of first love,
the miracles that wait for no one,
the enchantments of power, the politicians'

desecration of words, the Ponzi schemes,
the false hope of living without magic.
Yet why refuse to speak in the first,

not the second or third? And what possible
pleasure could there be in refusing
to speak without a voice of my own?

Failure

I tripped on the book, *Failure*, by Philip
Schultz, fluent in forgiveness, but struggling
to get the failure just right, I crossed out
words that echoed pity and spite; looked for

the opposite of justice and revenge;
waited for longing to turn out right;
and turned failure into a poem, instead,
though not entirely my own. *You look*

like a poet, he said. *White hair photographs*
well in this light. What had he seen in me?
What had he wanted to capture in snapping

my pic? Thick sunlight bursting through the blown
dead head of a failed poet, gone to seed, or
a dandelion blowing in the breeze?

In Twos

In twos, pairs, opposites — up, down, with, with-
out, such as a naked man trembling

by the wall in my backyard, covered in dirt,
saying how sorry he is. But a dark-eyed

cashier smiles and tells me to have a good one,
meaning a day, a life. Even the dying

dog and I are a pair. We overstay
our welcome, bicker, but side with fate,

thinking of putting each other down,
saying how similar we really are.

Even as we try to run away,
we know we won't get far, trembling

by a wall or cashing in our smiles,
the two of us zipped up in our body bags.

Emergency Ward

Poor little rich girl lifts her wrists and brings
the bandages into view. Also, cut
marks high up on her thighs. Torn hem of her
short skirt is cut down to size by the fingered

caress of her painted fingernails on
black band-aids. Trickles of blood from higher
up where the mess of the last caress lingers
under her gothic dress. She confesses

her symptoms for the dark transfusion
that slides into her veins and crawls towards
her pierced heart. The emergency ward

spins out a castle and the nurses are wearing
black stockings — fetishes of a healing
profession — nursing the goth girl in the dark.

The Poet as a Bear

At the Tango Palace, the poet is

a talking pooh bear. Lumbering,
he shambles in. *I eat my own mystery,*
he says, *so you can't find me.* Full of surprises,

but no wonder. Then filled with wonder,
but no surprises. Yet at the reading,
he rears, charges, bites into my head,

tears off the scalp, claws me down the face,
and rakes my chest. He gives me another
gift — this bearish poem and things bearlike.

He's telling me that the last guy he ate
left his cell phone in his hip pocket.
After the attack, he finds another

way to hide in the mystery of this poem.

Escaping Fate

Why does everything hinge on how the gate
swings open or shut, how it begins and ends
riding on a hasp with rusty bolts? Endurance
is the test and how it resolves itself, how it

all turns around or turns on you. Or in closing
shut, comes to a merciful or merciless end.
But before it does, let the fatal ties
slip from their moorings away from dry docks.

Haul anchor and tail, sail, fare forward, leave
oceanography to cartographers. You're a
mystic, not a mistake. Pray, dance. With the surge

of waves, lift off. Don't mock fate. Escape. Become
a seabird. The change wished for in dying is still death.
Why wish? Live life's transforming flight and fly, *fly*.

Making Peace

The fever pitch of the final grudge match
was a nervous collision of magicians.
Behind us on the highway, our mother
was bound and gagged. And if we lost her,

we'd lose everything. Hard feelings — between us,
but she refused to take it back — the one thing
we couldn't give her — our happiness,
or its faint possibility, like a murmuring heart.

And why aren't you happy for me? he asked
trembling, not looking at me sitting at the wheel.
And we set out on a new collision course —

life on its own terms — palpable, real, this time —
to straighten each other out after years of words.
So why couldn't we stop warring and make peace?

Pleading Innocence

Providence has a name — any name but ours.
The interview is over with keeping score:
Who got who a job, or pointed one out?
Who helped who when he refused to pick up

his bed and walk? But who keeps score
when the scorekeeper has a score to settle?
Beyond crying in his sleep with nothing at stake
because one of us is wrong and the other lost —

And one of us jests at the other's scars —
When you win the argument, you lose a brother.
And you finally have what you wanted

in the pull and push of heaven and earth —
the lullaby of the good life and a brother
you're not afraid to forgive, pleading innocence.

Making Friends Disappear

I'm a magician. I make my friends disappear.
Dexter was run down by a car and got dragged down
the road on our first day of high school.
Michael and Wayne were carelessly lost
when they took me for a last drink down
in the Marina and let me go — because
I had to — and one died and the other
went hunting for the sheer thrill of the kill.
Later still, I lost a friend when he said it
wasn't supposed to turn out like this, and that
he'd call me from the South Pacific,
but never did. I simply lost sight of them.
With the best trick of all, I made them
disappear and lost my dearest friends.

Don't Go Away Mad

Let go of your unkind illness. Let go
of your control and its many cruel needs.

Let go of this disorder to unleash sweet chaos
in the simplest terms — ungovernable

massacres of the way things are. Let go
of the blessings of madness and the wounds

of reason, chemical rage and radiation.
You were loved. You are loved. You will be loved.

Any glitch will have us in the last ditch.
Be careful what you wish for. I wished for it

before you, and I'm still brushing off the dirt.
I told you about my mother and my friends.

I told you how afraid I was— and angry.
Let go of your rage, they said. *Don't go away mad.*

Poet with Sunflower

A poet contemplates a sunflower —

He holds the white heat of the sun-scorched sky
in his unclenched eyes. The poet's villa is
a wilderness with a view of the unpossessed

sea. He lifts his head with the proud flower
to observe an ancient chariot
and rider cross the morning's threshold.

How, like a bloodied pen, he throws his spear
at the Adriatic. Threat hums along the coast.
A shark's fin vibrates through blood. In a hail

of seabirds, he climbs the rocks towards the
heliocentric sky. When the sunflower
lifts its head, its spine stands as straight as a man's —

the poet's stem and the flower's spine won't bend.

She Was Supposed to Die First

In my monastic, midnight room, pale grey
and white, I wait for my wife to fall asleep
to sit alone, late into the steadfast night.
White and grey carpets mirror the grey walls

and in the stilled, speckled light, liquor bottles
in my jewel-encrusted cabinet shine forth
with diamond light: Armagnac and brandy.
Sitting alone, reading *The New York Times*,

suffering for the sins of the world, dressed
in a pale blue caftan, wearing Jesus
sandals on my crossed feet, a half-empty glass,

of anything on the rocks, cradled in my hands.
This night, straight whiskey, no chaser.
And as she sleeps, I wonder who will die first.

Street Parade

An urban magician, I'm lost on my quest
for magic spaces and traces of defeat
in storm-stayed eyes — visions and blackouts.
I deface a poster for a women's shelter —

an Eastern icon on a graffiti wall.
In the fenced-off downtown core, cruisers burn.
Riot police beat their shields with magic batons
in 4/4 time. I'm spattered with stage blood.

My muse is looking for someplace trendy to eat,
and I'm on a gutless fast. She ignores my rants
at her own peril and turns away from

the conjurer's sense of reality.
Both of us drift down endless city streets —
in a parade of demystified lives.

THE SUBJECT IS COLOR

Rothko is already on Main Street.
His subject is color. A young girl
is huddled against a cold white wall.
He sees her as a sudden streak of red.

The swathe of color, like a nude,
unfurls a blushing, stolen kiss from her ruby red lips.
A spurt of blue splashes from her eyes,
declaring that night will go on forever.

The thawing gesture of her brushlike hand
squirts out the kind of color a painter
needs in his denial of *white*. Rothko

sees everything as yellow, red and blue.
In primary hues, he braves winter's cold
and blazes its blank canvas with bright paint.

Breathing Light

> *So let us go forward, quietly, each on his own path,*
> *forever making for the light.*
>   ~Vincent Van Gogh

1 Morning Star

Lark out of a wheat field breathes in yellow.

In the grainy light of keeping morning's
secret to become what you see, a sower
plants seeds of light at sunrise. Out of dark earth,

thin, flame-shaped seedlings in sheaves of light choose
to be like morning birds lifting to the sun.
Spinning off pinwheels of spangled light, brightness

hurls its sunflowers even into a mineshaft.
All is startled light waiting to be born.
In a cry of light, bright hues give birth to sight.

The combustion of the all-seeing sky
ignites new eyes that behold the living light.
A sun-headed sunrise is all the light we need

to breathe in what we see in fields of light.

2 Evening Star

Waking in a wheat field at night with shrieking crows,

a painter collects hues — chrome yellow and blue.
In a hymn to light, never lonely in walking
alone, he carries the song the lark sang

in his own throat. Alone, like the sower,
he is totally himself. In his light-bearing
eyes, dark fields shine forth with flowers of light.

The sunflowers of his perplexity turn
night's lamentation into remembrance —
scent of linseed oil, taste of sunflower seeds,

breath of fresh light. In the wheeling of the stars,
his art swirls, ripens, breathes in the wheat field.
In the night sky, seed-shaped flames alight in the act

of painting darkness with blazing starlight.

Enchantments of the Real World

The Play of the World

What do you mean give up my illusions?

What about the magical links between
my brain and the storm of the century?
Finally, it works the way I want it to —

My delusions pull all the unseen strings,
set up a correspondence with the other world.
How extraordinary the ordinary

is—an encounter with the mystery of the world.
An unconcealed weapon points the way there.
It's not the same as revealing the threat.

The storm is freighted with dead pigeons.
To find myself already in the world, playing
hide-and-seek with transmigrating spirits,

the miracle play of the *enchantments* of the world.

Appearing in the Wilderness

A magician leaves the stage in a puff
of smoke, appears in a box of trees, wearing
buckskin. He points his wand and hangs the moon
in the sky — a *trompe l'oeil* backcloth. He sets out
on a wilderness tour across the cold
country. A time to free his mind from magic.
In scant moonlight, he zaps the wilderness.
A grizzly now wears his discarded cape —
his red-lined Domino and silk top hat.
With his paw, the bear makes the spawning
salmon leap in the mountain's magic stream.
The magician, his body wrapped in bear-skin,
follows the dancing bear on a tightrope —
high in the performing sky — a moon ray.

Hunger

Light drifts like wild smoke across an empty sky.
The magician drags his hunger, like an arctic
fox, through ravening snow. Over snowbound
terrain, the wizard wind pursues him to the edge

of a mound of stranded rocks. He lies flat
against cold, hard ground. Then vanishes into
a rift of spruce trees. Along the mountain ridge,
standing motionless, a blur follows his escape.

He sees himself in the fox, northern magician.
Boulders huddle together — like hibernating
dancing bears. Nature holds up the whole shebang.

Only the fox can see the strings, pulleys and levers.
The landscape is a stage. The magician,
covered in fur, changes into his animal disguise.

Motion Sickness

The opening passage is not a true beginning.
I'm no longer looking for enchantment
but shelter from the storm. Leave-taking
implies momentum, torque, thrust. An imperfect

movement — a bend in the road — going on,
tuned to the emotion of perpetual
motion. But how does a magician
trace annihilation — the fizzling out

of purpose, the diminished will, the last
performance, especially when crossing
the morning's frontier? The storm vanishes

in a tailwind — a tailspin. I keep travelling.
To pick up speed, I persuade myself
that it's not motion sickness but real emotion.

Field Notes

To explore the wilderness, I keep field
notes on small white flowers and red berries.
I ignore the spirit world at my own peril.
Attached to winter grief, a lonely hand

holds a rigged-up notebook.
In failing light, words voyage across a blank
page — a lonesome bird in a flying field.
The pencil jots down arrivals and departures,

as if they hold obscure meanings of their own.
Last time and the time before it was
the end of an old arrangement and the

beginning of a new one. Time to stay alone
in the honeymoon rooms of motels and cabins.
Our ghosts hum in each bed slept in without sleep.

A Spear Thrown at the Gathering Storm

Often lost on the Trans-Canada Highway,
remote places appear as drifting forests.

In massive drifts, the wilderness floats by.
In squalls, a snowman practises his vanishing act.

To get rid of weapons, except for the ones
a warrior conceals, he throws a spear

at the gathering storm. Small towns, lakes and rivers
feel the wound he jests at. Harrowing clouds

part and manifest the mountains.
But hiding behind the need for freedom,

muscles twitch along the throat and surrender
to the storm. Night tries to erase the loss from view —

to deposit its victims on the shore;
to drop its weapons made of bone and hair.

Changing Landscapes

In changing landscapes, a lone magician
conceives of himself as a wildlife
photographer, wilderness warrior,
explorer, tree-hugger, and human companion

to wolves and bears. As if the transformation
happens somewhere — there — or it will never
happen — ever. He thinks he's an animal.
They're unconvinced. He travels. They defy

the burden of stillness. On a cold road,
he wonders what their conception is of him —
lonesome traveller, wildlife photographer,

gutted prey, walking food, stuffed toy —
its tangled string strung from a Sequoia —
or just another magician in the forest.

Inward Journey

Enchantments of the animal kingdom
trick us into believing we will survive
the way the wolf and bear do — this deception
in nature spoils the inward journey —

But on the road we find a way to find our way.
Learn to move and sense the movement
beneath the clothes, beneath the skin, muscle and bone.
If we need to rest, we rest. But drifting needs

no rest. The wicked ways of highways and byways
offer consolation for finding ourselves there.
Nowhere is where we want to be — where the road leads.

To wish to God we had not gone there
is to wish to God we had not been there.
But we were there and travelled the same road.

Magic Forest

Memory steps over my fallen friends.
I choose a new identity in the new world.
I stand in a hall of trees — Sequoias
and Douglas Firs. I enter the rare book-
room of the forest's great library —
archives that reek of Lodgepole Pine, Yellow Aspen,
Pacific Dogwood, and Trembling Cedar.
Forgive me for not dreaming about trees till now.
In my striving, I can't double back,
can't fold in on myself to collapse the past,
reverse the trajectory. Now, the ghostly coast
appears. I'm turning into what I see —
the dwelling place of all generations —
the port that waits to identify me.

Winter Photograph

What is it that I reserve for myself
beyond the mysteries of the body —
giving up incantation for photography,
avoidance and indirection for action?

Still in wonder, my dark lens is snow-blind.
Snow obstructs the windshield and rearview.
A winter mirage mocks the set-up and shot
with: *That's no way to shoot the wilderness.*

Tired of following logging trucks and semis,
the lost trail leads back to the same spot.
I shoot photos by the side of the road.

With enough film to document the trip,
in rough images, I look like a dancing
polar bear eating a camera.

The Farther Away He Journeys

A travelling magician lets silence in

without discarding it — a way of turning things
around, deepen within and erase the atmosphere.
Darkly growing in punctured lungs, silence

affects the battle, drenches the skin with animal scent.
The stopovers are last exits, winding back —
the reversal in nature — Trips won't last.

The farther away he journeys, the closer
he comes to the edge of freedom. To keep
from arguing with the dead, he lets it claim

him and separate him from the past,
as if he's made a suicide pact,
convinced the journey must end this way,

but at the last moment can't go through with it.

The Other Shore

The moment defines what I'm doing here.
Reluctant to leave everything behind —
to destroy the book of potions — I consider
how free I am. But the moment burns off

the mist and haze. Long distances make me
distant; remote. The wilderness heads out
like a charging bear — against its puppet prey.
After years spent yearning for this place,

often leaning towards another,
it's suddenly *there* — the locus, the point
sought after, but soon avoided.

Then not knowing what to do, or where to go,
in case I fall backwards in the descent,
without magic, I lean towards the other shore.

Reading the River

The river is within us...
~T. S. Eliot

What I don't understand runs through me
like a river. Never the same twice, it flows,
flashes, surges, slows. From a mountain spring,
it runs through me in a river capture
of memory and dreams — river of lost
time, longing, grief. Haven for river folk,
it longs to reach beyond the estuary.
A newborn river, like the young Mississippi,
runs through me. Long-legged waterbirds lift off.
Catfish rise and fall to the sounds of a harp,
whistle and flute. Raindrops fall at the same instant
in the atmospherics of river weather.
I untie the sailor's knot of grief and swim free.
What I long for flows through me like a river.

Now, the dervishes dance on the riverbank
with musicians playing on a riverboat
carrying them along. Shouting and calling
from the water to the shore and back again —
the voices of the river talk together,
rising and taking possession of every throat
and tongue. And at night, there is music and wild
dancing by firelight. On the dancing
ground, more celebrations sprout up along
the waterway. In the trance of the river,
the dancers lift up to the roar of the river

dance. It moves in meandering, and everything moves
with it, and the river runs through us
and beyond us, and the river's theme is peace.

I belong here, dancing to the river's song —
I belong to art and time in the language
of the currents, playing the game of flashing waters
in the miracle of river life —
the mystery of fording the river and stepping,
refreshed, cleansed, onto the beckoning shore.
I belong here with otters, turtles, ducks and frogs.
Gulls orient me. I read the river's ancient
scrolls that hint at my destination. In faring
forward, the river's spirit will preserve me.
Delighting in what I can't understand,
I'm at peace with the infinite jests of the river
that lift me with water wings. I'm gifted
with gratitude, rafting on the rivers of the world.

Walking Naked

In the rawness of being together,
lying naked is a form of concealment,

not intimacy. Skin, bruised as rotten
fruit — like a warrior whose armor

is skin-deep. Naked surface tension
and arcs of longing, our youthful drive

is spurred on by the late 70s.
With the goad of free love, the music

preaches hurt — yet not for throat singers
who breathe heady ozone. Like their ancestors,

they breathe in isolation. But the magic
this morning predicts fatal light.

As they walk along the horizon, they sing
how easy it is to become a naked target.

Arrivals and Departures

The frozen architecture points the way
to Alaska. In locating traces
of an unassumed road, I find I'm lost.
A hinged sign taunts me with *Use at your own
risk*. The mountain road is longer than
the one I dreamed of. I keep travelling
to avoid arriving. Narwhals drift
in ice formations. Tusks lift to meet
my shifting gaze. I calculate the risk
of being able to get through. Fear bites
into my face and sinks its canines
into my determination to arrive.
I have to *arrive* when travelling,
and not travel simply to arrive.

For Those Who Watch the Wilderness

For those who watch the wilderness,
willows, alders, birch and spruce lift off
to capture the sky. The wilderness drifts
westward to the mountain fortress to join
the trees. Birch bark scrolls and annals narrate
where the journey begins and ends. Written
on bark in the forest's great library,
reality is wilderness literature,
the story of births and deaths — the secret
history of those that watch the wilding
and those that record what they've seen and where
they've been — their eyes searching the wilderness
for the life of the lake inscribed on leaves
of the towering, tree-lined bookshelves.

West Coast Messages

If I make it, I'll find myself on the West Coast
where oceanic messages are sent
and sometimes received in code, saying:
You're going the wrong way.

I must decipher what's become of this quest.
As I reach a last minute destination,
a lake completely locked in ice,
distant mountains that turn on me,

bend and fold before my constant gaze.
The Rockies lean towards my snow blindness.
And if I can't get to the mountains, with no Sherpa

to guide me, a Polar bear drifts down
on a raft of melting ice. A white rainbow behind
rears up to deliver a message: *Come back to life.*

The Secret Language of the Hunt

In a mountain session, memories
hide in cliffs and jags where ravens nest
with feathers plucked by Arctic wind; ice-hands.
They remind me of why I left home;

why I slept in motels and why, in running
away from eastern lawns, I sought another
landscape. Highways travel inside you.
But along high mountain ridges, forests,

scrublands, or along open plains, only
white wolves follow my near escape and reveal
the secret language of the hunt. Moose,

caribou, and even porcupines dream
of Alaskan wolves and aerial hunting.
And, in my hidden life, wolves bear me away.

Winter's Phantoms

Beneath ballooning down, Mira holds on.
A white-mantled avalanche shakes itself
off. Awake, it shambles down the mountainside,
trips through the Kootenays and rolls on

in the southeast. As she reads phantom letters
inscribed on the rock face, she comes across
survivors of a train derailment.
Asleep in white drifts, winter's ghosts

tempt her to join them in the haunting.
But when the rearing mountain discards
its snowy cape along the trail, the landmass

collects the tingling energy of another
ghost. Mira's specter shifts from foothold
to foothold and joins winter's phantoms.

Substitutions

When I substitute names and places, I replace
place names with other substitutes. They are
placeholders for undiscovered sites. Let one thing stand
in for another. But then, just before

leaving what remains of the mountain trails
for the West Coast, I substitute the word
mountain for sky and *road for rain.* And in
a last ditch attempt to unify it all,

in nature's summary of the plan, in a sentence
that has no beginning and no real end, I replace
the word *Whale* with the ancient word for *God.*

And fall on my knees to pray to the in-
escapable divinity of the real world
where the holy is made visible.

Abandoning the Page

The opening passage tells of the long,
sheltering night rolling in on moonlight.
In quick rotations of the killing eye,
snow geese, on the verge of abandoning

ice fields, sink into your rifle's jewelled scope.
Unimpeded by mountains, ravens call out.
From my black-skinned notebook, new words fly up
to greet sounds winging across the lingual lake.

I'm writing about winter birds that circle
overhead in the image and likeness
of tundra swans and ptarmigan. Across the

turquoise sky, snow geese crisscross in long V-
formations. And the rushing of winged words
abandons the fields of this vast page.

Driftwood Fire

Wreathed in the thin, black smoke of a driftwood
fire, scattered pages from a book of potions
drift towards Port Dover beach — a friend's summer
house on the lake. A month of Sundays,

but no one remembers drowning in the guest
room lined with old books. Still starving in bed,
everything begins and ends with bedroom notes.
Nobody draws attention to the words

of what they're saying and what was once unsaid.
So that when they say *lake* or *fire*, the record
shows only what the words look like on the page,

not in the mind. Now, the words *driftwood fire*
flare up, stranded in a cold place miles away
from the black smoke of a driftwood fire.

THE DESCENT

Falling into the crevasse breaks your spell.
In the sheer drop down the side of the cliff

in a programmed sequence, night is coming on.
Hinged to aching muscles, the loaded rifle

rests unbroken in the clench of scarred hands.
A bullet in the chamber finds its target.

The ricochet sets your alibi back
two more days. Is this what you planned: to drop

her body off a spur of rock, to shear it off,
like something that you simply have to kill?

Shadows creep along the mountain pass.
You're determined to do it in the face

of the enemy and search for a place
to bury this wish, like other ashes.

Throat Singers of the Animal Kingdom

The words of the song said: *Keep travelling.*

On the way, we got married in a forest church.
But the lost highway I was looking for
wasn't along the lifeline, but closer —

a misdirection, not a trick revealed.
In a stand of sequoias, a congregation
of birds flew out singing aboriginal hymns.

Guessed at, the harmonies were unknown to us.
Ravens left their nests, like abandoned pews.
They blew the bride and groom a morning song.

The wedding guests were flocks of migrating birds.
Once heard, the music could only be inscribed
on our avian throats or along our lupine

tongues — throat singers of the animal kingdom.

Burning Lake

On the honeymoon, Johanna says the lake
rained down on the tundra and tumbled down
from an ancient molten sky that landed
on this deserted airstrip. Designed and built
by glacial engineers, it stretched out
for miles and miles in every direction.
And in white heat, it rode along burning
circles in wide rims — flaming spawn and wrack.

She says translucent fish with smaller ones
in their guts once swam beneath these ancient
waters. She's looking up to see a torrent
of deep sky flaring and falling in flames —
burning lake of prehistoric fire.
We swim in reflections of blazing sky.

Landscape of Endings

Another lost highway. The sky: starless,
indecipherable, amnesiac.

I wanted her to forget — I showed her
the palm of my hand and pointed to the route.

An illusionist was looking to be
a shaman, a medicine man, a wood spirit.

Scribbled in glacial notebooks,
my original name — *lost magician* —

that marked unknown places on the map
and stretched pelts on poles. Improvised shelter

against sure death. For trade, gathered shells, bones,
and caribou antlers. And left alone,

collected what sunless skies had tossed down
long ago on a landscape of endings.

Mountain Outlook

From the mountain outlook, the first wave
ploughs the wilderness. Hoes rows and furrows
of the first cause. Draws circles in blazing
starlight. Builds runes and ruins on a wilderness

farm. Frames sets and subsets of stars and crystals,
mountain ranges and coastlines. Light presses
everything together and then pulls it apart.
Mirrored in projected star wheels, the wilderness

spins out of the word n-o-r-t-h-w-e-s-t. It bowls over
mountains with rays of living light. Pieces
break and slide off the jagged edge. Blood lisps

from the magician's body, nailed to the mountain-
side. The next wave moves from the mountain out-
look, hoeing rows and furrows to plough the wilderness.

The First Tree We Ever Climbed

When we were young, we made crosses from the first
tree we ever climbed together. And carried

the sorrow of genesis in our bodies:
the grief of the three-day ending and killing

of trees and each other. Now, we glide down
from the peak in a landslide of shrieking

ravens and disappear. But we almost
leave without recalling the heights planted

with crosses. We've robbed the grave of the mountain
god, sacked caves and temples, brought back relics

and scrolls from the mountaintop, but never
built an altar or learned how to love other

species. No longer young, we glide down the mountain
at last to know and fathom our true worth.

WHALE WATCHING

My only pleasure now is watching whales
in the Pacific Ocean. Lost in mist
at sunset on a blue sightseeing boat,
against the spray on the bow, the rest
of the whale watchers are covered in yellow
raincoats and matching hats. Like a tourist
visiting a shrine, I pray to the whales
and escape the implications of what
the trip has meant. When suddenly off the West
Coast Pacific, the entire continent
shifts, tilts, tips and moves towards a whale's slit-eyed
gaze. Its blowhole spouts off about survival
in whale song. But like the weather, I quickly turn.
Watching eyes ride with the all-seeing whales.

Enchantments of the Open Road

North, north — that was all I could think of.
But to end there was not the end. I almost
drifted away without remembering
moonlight sculling on the lake and the loon

telling me what was happening. But that
was the summer of many summers ago,
before finding my *soul* on the open road.
And when I arrived at the Pacific shore

with no news of you from either coast,
I almost went away without recalling
where I was supposed to be. And, enchanted

by the lone raven's cry, in the wilding
of the wilderness and the mystery of the world,
how on the road, grief leads to gratitude.

ANTHONY LABRIOLA's work has appeared in such publications as *The Canadian Forum, PRISM international, Lo Straniero, Vallum: New International Poetics, Still Point Arts Quarterly,* and *Passion: Poetry.* He has had several collections of poetry published, including two by Shanti Arts—the other being *Birds and Arrows* (2017).

Labriola was born in Italy but grew up in Canada. He comes from a large family, and many of his siblings are artists. He is married to his childhood sweetheart, Louisa Josephine. They have five grown children—each is an artist in his or her own right.

Labriola's love of poetry began at a young age when he first read Dylan Thomas's *The Force That Through the Green Fuse Drives the Flower*. The same force drove him to write and write and write with a focus on mystical realities. The theater also held a strange fascination for him, and he acted in, directed, and wrote many plays. After graduating high school in the late 1960s, he studied English and French at the University of Toronto. Bent on teaching literature and the arts, he received a B. Ed. in English and Dramatic Arts from the Faculty of Education, and an M.A. from the Graduate Center for the Study of Drama. He taught English, Drama and Performing Arts for thirty-two years. He was also Curriculum Chair in the Arts and was inspired by the talents of his students.

Labriola now lives in Toronto, Ontario, Canada and teaches Life Writing at Seneca College.

Shanti Arts

Nature • Art • Spirit

Please visit us on online
to browse our entire book catalog,
including poetry collections and fiction,
books on travel, nature, healing, art,
photography, and more.

Also take a look at our highly
regarded art and literary journal,
Still Point Arts Quarterly, which
may be downloaded for free.

www.shantiarts.com

www.ingramcontent.com/pod-product-compliance
Lightning Source LLC
Chambersburg PA
CBHW070450050426
42451CB00015B/3416